Mariana sighed, cradling the warm coffee cup in her hands. Slow clouds of steam rose from it in irregular patterns that, had she been paying attention to them, could resemble cotton candy. But her mind was elsewhere, her gaze fixated on the window of the cozy coffee shop she was in. Raindrops collided with the window, their tip tap sound becoming hypnotizing and making Mariana completely forget about the passage of time.

When she took a sip from her cup, it had grown slightly cold. She drank it anyway, lamenting her tendency for being absentminded. Mariana's eyes traveled from the window to the phone resting on the table, and another sigh escaped her lips at the lack of new notifications. She didn't need to be a genius to figure out that she'd been stood up. Maybe her date had a good reason for not giving her an explanation, maybe not, it would only have been their second date, so Mariana supposed that she was in no position to request any sort of excuse.

Nonetheless, she hoped that the guy was okay, even if she had no intentions of rescheduling. Again.

Her nails tapped on the surface of the table, following the rhythm of the rain which had become more intense. She'd forgotten her umbrella at home and didn't feel like running under the storm unnecessarily. It wasn't like she had anywhere else to go for the day, Mariana thought.

Mariana bit her lip, grabbed her phone to unlock the screen with a swipe and sent a text to her date, just in case.

Everything alright?

And then, just to avoid sounding more serious than she wanted to sound, Mariana sent an emoji of a worried face, or what appeared to be that. The text was delivered, but her date's last connection had been two hours ago. Mariana grunted, wondering if she'd dare going on a hunt on other social media apps for any update.

"Am I that desperate?", she mumbled to herself. Mariana finished her cold coffee and decided that no, she wasn't. At least not yet. If only she'd brought a book with herself, that way she would have a way of passing the time that didn't involve her phone until the rain stopped.

Her stomach grunted. Mariana would have bought a slice of cake earlier if she hadn't been waiting for someone else, and now she avoided ordering only for herself after telling the waiter that she needed a table for two. Well, she could always say that it really was a table for three. Me, myself and I, she thought. A curse flew out of her lips, Mariana was feeling second hand embarrassment for herself.

She placed the cup on the table and then let her head fall into her hands, muffling a tired groan. The sound of ceramic against wood made her look up to see a waiter leaving a plate in front of her. It had a single chocolate chip cookie on it.

"I didn't order this", Mariana said.

"I know", the waiter replied. The guy, seemingly her age and taller that he probably was from the angle Mariana was looking up at him, readjusted his green apron nervously. The apron had a sticker that said 'hi! my name's devon' and the lack of capitalization made one of her eyebrows go up. "It's on the house, you seem like you need it".

Mariana cringed, "that obvious?". The guy nodded. "Ugh, if only it stopped raining, just for a couple of minutes. I live, like, four blocks away from here".

The guy, Devon, shuffled his feet. "My shift ends in half an hour or so".

"Cool", Mariana said, not knowing how to reply.

Devon scratched the back of his head. "What I mean is, well, I also live nearby so we could share my umbrella. I'm guessing you don't have one".

"Not with me, no", Mariana sighed. "Look, thanks, dude, but I'd rather not let a stranger know where I live, okay?".

She didn't want to offend him either, but it was better being safe rather than sorry. Devon was taken aback by her words, but then realization came to him. "Seems fair, I hadn't thought of it that way".

"It's alright".

"Can I pick up the cup?", Devon pointed to it, to which Mariana nodded. He left with the cup and she ate the cookie. It was soft on the inside, still warm as if recently made. By the time she finished with it, the rain was stopping. Mariana left a tip of the same value of the cookie and left, looking back to see Devon cleaning her table and waving goodbye at her. She waved back.

Back at home, she checked her phone and saw that her text remained unanswered. Oh, well, his loss. Mariana went on with her life, she had some test to study for.

Next week, Mariana went back to the coffee shop with a couple of textbooks and her laptop. Thankfully, the weather forecast said it would be sunny all day long. Devon, who was behind the cash register that day, welcomed her with a smile.

"Table for two?", he joked. Mariana blew a raspberry at him.

"Table for a lonely studying soul", she explained, placing her books and laptop on a nearby table. "Give me a cup of your strongest coffee, I want to stay awake for this".

Devon charged her for a black coffee, but when he brought it to her table, he also gave her another chocolate chip cookie, insisting it was on the house. "Consider it a 'good luck on your test' gift. I eat at least one every day and pass mine with honors".

"What's your major?", Marian asked before she bit into the cookie. "Mine's biology".

"Mechanical engineering". Devon was about to say something else, but one of his coworkers called for him. "Gotta go, talk to you later?", he asked with a hopeful note in his voice.

Mariana smiled, "sure thing". She dove right back into her books, took notes and almost fell asleep twice by the time the coffee shop begun emptying. She picked up her things and was preparing to leave when a drop fell, then another. "Damn you, weather forecast", she said as she saw the rain fall down on the street.

Devon laughed behind her, so Mariana turned around to see him. The guy held an umbrella in his hand. "Forgot yours again?". She nodded. "Well, the offer still stands, y'know?"

Marian laughed, "alright, fine, you win". Devon smiled brightly at her. "But only because I don't want my things ruined".

They walked close to one another, trying to stay as dry as they could, and sharing funny stories about being tired college students that didn't get enough sleep. When they reached Mariana's place, Devon said, "next time, I'll take you to the park if it's not raining".

Mariana raised an eyebrow, "I don't know, going to the park with a stranger?"

"What about a friend?", Devon offered, letting Mariana add him as a contact on her phone.

Mariana accepted, the lingering thought of the guy becoming something more setting itself on the back of her mind. Later, when she decided to give it more consideration, Mariana found herself rather happy with the possibility.

*Maybe being stood up isn't always
a bad thing.*
~Mariana

Corner Coffee Shop

STORY OF MARIANA